I am...

Powerful.

Strong.

Loved.

Enough.

Self- love Publishing

Copyright © 2018 by Michelle Anderson

All rights reserved.

Printed in the United States of America

978-0-692-12819-0

Published by Self Love

Clinton Twp. Michigan

selfloveexperience@gmail.com

All scripture is taken from the New International Version

All rights reserved. No part of this publication may be reproduced, distributed, or transmitted in any form or by any means, including photocopying, recording, or other electronic or mechanical methods, without the prior written permission of the publisher, except in the case of brief quotations embodied in critical reviews and certain other noncommercial uses permitted by copyright law.

Editing contributions by Angelica Jackson, Maria Romain and Valisa Murray.

Art contributions by A.lex.is Frank.lin

Cover illustration Shutterstock

Phenomenal Woman poem by Maya Angelou (1978)

Dedication

To my daughters, Angelica and Savanna Rose, who exude strength that they have yet to discover. To my friends who supported and encouraged me along the way.

To two young women that I have had the pleasure of having in my life, Kelsey and Brittney. May you young ladies always remember that your identity and worth come from God.

TABLE OF CONTENTS

INTRODUCTION
My identity---6
Fear--7
You are enough--14
Forgiveness--22
Honoring your body---29
Letters---30
Goals---34
Proud---37
Happy---38
Grateful--39
Love---41
I am unashamed--45
In mw weakness--48
Dear Self---52
I will quit--53
INFLUENCES---54
Prayers---55
Women who inspire you--59
What makes me beautiful--60
What God has called me to do---63
WHO AM I? ---65
God's Word---68
I give myself permission ---78
I am thankful---80
I am a phenomenal women--81
Gods truth--85
Their Stories ---91
Begin Journaling, "I AM STATEMENTS" --------------------------94
A letter to my past ---136
Authors Motivation---138

Introduction

Have you ever asked yourself, who am I? Who or what defines who I am? I often wondered where my own identity came from? As a child growing up, I was referred to as stupid, ugly and fat by my peers as well as adults in my life and I believed it. I believed the lie. I was never told that I was smart, I was beautiful, or enough.

I grew up in a home without biological ties to my mother and father. By the time I was three years old, I was separated from my parents and my siblings and placed into foster care. It was stated on documentation that I found, that after my parents completed a parenting class, we would've been able to return home. Needless to say, we never returned to our parents. So, to add to my thoughts of being stupid, ugly and fat, after I found these documents, I felt unwanted.

My siblings and I were placed in different foster homes until we were reunited by the woman who I learned to call grandma. She made the decision to open her heart and home and adopt the three of us. I went from being in a two parent (my mother and father) home, to several foster homes and lastly to my adoptive home (my grandmother).

From birth to age three my world had changed. These should have been the years I received nurturing and love. These should have been the years that I learned to build healthy attachments and trusting relationships. Instead, these were the years that I learned to detach myself from everyone except my siblings. As I grew, the memory of my mother began to fade. Who was she?

This was the foundation that caused me to constantly question my identity. If I did not know my mother or father, how would I ever know who I was (so I thought)? "Who am I?", was the question I silently asked myself. I never really knew who I was or where I fit in. Most kids in my neighborhood were being raised by both mother and father. That wasn't my story.

You see, growing up I was taught that the woman raising me was my grandmother, I thought she was my father's mother. By the time I was 16, I learned this not to be true. I learned that the man I thought was my father, was actually my sister's father and not mine. My oldest brother and I had a different father. So again, I asked the question, "who am I?" Another question was added to my long list. That question was, "who is my father?"

Could you imagine learning that the man you thought was your father, really wasn't? I didn't see him often, but he was the only dad I knew. After learning this, I began to experience so many emotions as a teen. I began to feel anger, confusion, rejection and betrayal. Growing up I had experienced several forms of abuse, including verbal and sexual. If I were living with my biological parents, this wouldn't have happened, would it? They would have protected me, right?

After a certain age I had no remembrance of my mother at all, the only thing I knew was her name. Every Sunday I would search the obituaries for her. I was so excited each week when I didn't find her name amongst those who had passed away. This gave me hope that she was still alive. Maybe one day I could meet her, learn about her and in turn, learn of myself.

During my search for my identity, the one thing I could turn to was journaling. Journaling was the way that I expressed my feelings and my thoughts. In my home, children were to be seen and not heard. How could I ever say what was on my mind? How could I ever be heard if I was always silenced? I could never use the voice that God had given me. How I felt never mattered. My thoughts and opinions were locked away in the pages of whatever notebook I could find.

You may also have many journals, just as I did. I encourage you to use this journal/workbook as a tool to discover who you are and who God has created you to be. Each page is meant for you to reflect on areas such as fear, your present, your past, your goals, forgiveness and most importantly, to help remind you of your value. As you go through this journal/workbook, consider what Gods word says about you. Do your own thoughts match his thoughts towards you?

I eventually learned who my biological parents were. Did they save me? No. Did they fill a void? No. Did they help me to learn who I was? No. I learned who they were, but it didn't help me with my own identity. I learned that it didn't matter who they were. Who they were and who I was were totally different people. We had different views on life, different experiences and different callings.

As I grew closer to God, I learned that my identity could only come from him. I was so busy yearning for my parents that I should have been seeking God. I believe that there was a reason he had us apart for so long. I honestly don't believe that I would have been the woman that I am today if my biological parents had raised me. God had a plan for me long before I was in my mother's womb. He knew that I would endure some heartache, but he also knew the heartache I endured would lead me to a passion for helping others. As you go through this journal/workbook, you will read about more of my personal experiences and be asked to reflect on your own. Use this as a tool and a guide to self-discovery and healing.

Remember, no matter what you have gone through and no matter what others have said about you, you are powerful, you are strong, you are loved, and you are enough! You are who God says that you are. You must replace any negative thinking with what God says. You were created in his image and after his likeness. He makes no mistakes. Your identity can only come from the Creator.

Happy Journaling,

Michelle Anderson

Each Day,
Finding My Voice.
Finding My Value.
Finding My Identity.
Finding Me.
I am Enough!

My Identity

My Identity can't be taken away

And can't be defined by others.

It doesn't come and go based on relationships or friendships.

My identity comes from God.

I am who he says that I am.

Fear. It can be your worst enemy or your greatest motivation!

Fear

Will you allow fear to stop you from being or doing what God has created you to do? At times, we may not know or walk in our identity due to fear.

We think to ourselves, *"Was that really God speaking to me?" "God could not have said that, I am too old, too young, not capable or not skilled enough."*

"It is no way this is who I am, others told me different, what if I fail?"

Jeremiah 1:5 states, "Before I formed you in the womb I knew you, before you were born I set you apart..."

In the book of Jeremiah, God spoke to Jeremiah and said, *"I am your creator, before you were born, I chose you."*

"I want you to go out into the nations and whatever I tell you, I want you to say it."

Jeremiah doubted himself. *"I'm not a good speaker and I'm too young."* He was afraid.

God reached out and touched his mouth and said,

"You are not too young, if I tell you to go then go. I will be with you and I will keep you safe, do not be afraid."

God sent Jeremiah out with authority to speak to the people to tell them of the things to come. God used Jeremiah, despite what he felt his ability was.

Whatever it is that you want to do or that God is calling for you to do, know that he has already given you what you need to fulfill his call. Do not doubt yourself. God will be with you.

What is it that you want to do or believe you are called by God to do and you are afraid to do?

These are the things I am afraid to say…

I know that getting them out by speaking them or writing them down will help me to be free. It is okay for me to be afraid, but it is not ok to be held captive by fear.

Fear can...

- *Stop you*
- *Paralyze you*
- *Dictate your actions*
- *Hold you hostage*
- *Rule over you*

Don't let it! Fear is a weapon of the enemy. He uses it to keep you from fulfilling God's purpose in your life. Use the weapons that God has given to you such as faith and courage to fight against fear.

What does Deuteronomy 31:6 say?

_____

_____

_____

_____

_____

_____

_____

_____

_____

_____

_____

_____

_____

What does Joshua 1:7-9 say?

Positive Reflection: Study scriptures on fear.

"Our Deepest Fear is not that we are inadequate. Our deepest fear is that we are POWERFUL beyond measure. It is our light, not our darkness that most frightens us. We ask ourselves, who am I to be brilliant, gorgeous, talented, and fabulous? Who are you not to be? You are a child of God. Your playing small does not serve the world. There is nothing enlightened about shrinking so that other people will not feel insecure around you, we are all meant to shine, as children do. We were born to make manifest the glory of God that is within us. It is not just in some of us, it is in everyone, and as we let our own light shine, we unconsciously give others permission to do the same. As we are liberated from our own fear, our presence automatically liberates others."

Marianne Williamson

You Are Enough

"Today Know that you are good enough.

Stop worrying if you are pretty enough,

Strong enough,

Rich enough,

Smart enough,

You must know that you are enough.

Don't let men (people) have power over you…

Take a deep breath and know that you matter, and you are ENOUGH"

Heather Stillufsen

"Just think,

You are here not by chance,

But by God's choosing.

His hand formed you

And made you the person you are.

He compares you to no one else.

You are one of a kind,

You lack nothing that his grace cannot give you.

He has allowed you to be here at this time in history to fulfill his special purpose for this generation."

    Roy Lessin

I have purpose and I will not be afraid to walk in it.

I will not allow others to dictate my purpose, I will allow God to lead me.

I am no longer the victim, I am victorious.

I am Chosen.

"But you are a chosen people, a royal priesthood, a holy nation, God's special possession…" (1 Peter 2:9 NIV)

Growing up, I did not think I had any gifts or talents. I had no clue what I was good at or what I would do with my life. Whatever gifts I may have had, were never cultivated. I was always told that I was just average. Because I was convinced that you, I was just average, I didn't work very hard. I didn't think I had any strengths. Seeking out my gifts was not something I was interested in doing. It wasn't until I listened to the voice of God that I realized my gifts and talents. I learned that I had the gifts of helps, teaching and serving.

Do you know your gifts and talents? Reflect on them and write them below.

_____

_____

_____

_____

_____

_____

_____

_____

_____

_____

_____

_____

_____

_____

_____

_____

Forgiveness

Forgiveness. *One of the hardest things I ever had to do. Forgive the family members who sexually and mentally abused me. Forgive the mother who could not provide for me. Forgive the kids who called me ugly and stupid as a child and forgive myself for believing the lies that were told to me instead of believing God's truth. I challenge you to choose to begin the process of forgiveness for yourself.*

Today I will choose to forgive, not because the people apologized or admitted what they did to hurt me. I forgive because God has forgiven me. I forgive because it exemplifies God's love.

Matthew 6:14 states that if I forgive others, God will forgive me.

These are the people I choose to forgive today:

1. _____

2. _____

3. _____

4. _____

5. _____

6. _____

Add to the list as needed.

Think to yourself, "do I forgive the way God forgives?"

Let's see what Scripture says…

Colossians 3:13 says

_____

_____

_____

_____

_____

_____

_____

_____

_____

Matthew 18: 21-22 says:

_____

_____

_____

_____

_____

_____

_____

_____

These are the steps I can take to forgive…

1. *Speak the offense out loud (e.g. I have not forgiven my uncle because he touched me inappropriately).*
   -How can you heal, if the offense is never revealed? (Ephesians 5:8-14, Jeremiah 6:14)
2. *Determine how you feel (I feel angry because he touched me).*
3. *Feel it (Feel it in an appropriate way. Do not try to mask it or hide it. Kick, scream, shout, get it out).*
4. *Now that you have acknowledged your feelings, what are you going to do with them next? How are you going to handle them? Do you want to continue being angry? (Ephesians 4:31-32)*

Remember, Jesus took all sins to the cross. Why do we continue to carry around our sins as well as the sins of others?

(Read this out loud to yourself or speak it to someone who needs to hear it.)

Today is the day that I stop allowing my scars to hurt me. Today is the day that I unapologetically decide to heal and to forgive. Unforgiveness will no longer hold me hostage.

"In the shadow of my hurt,
Forgiveness feels like a decision
to reward my enemy.
But in the shadow of the cross,
Forgiveness is merely a gift from
One undeserving soul to another."
Andy Stanley

Today I Choose…

- *To forgive*
- *To love*
- *To be happy*
- *Joy*
- *Peace*
- *To honor my body*

There were times in my life when my choices did not honor my body or God. I allowed my body to be used up and abused by men. I did not confuse love with sex, however it gave me the time and attention that I desired. This is something that I went through from not knowing my identity or worth. Our bodies were not designed to be used up by man but to be used by God.

1 Corinthians 6:19-20 states that my body is a temple. I will honor God with my body.

These are the things you can do today to honor God with my body…

1. Eat foods that are good for my body.
2. Exercise to keep my body strong.
3. Honor my body spiritually with fasting and prayer.
4. _____
5. _____
6. _____
7. _____
8. _____
9. _____
10. _____

Letters

Dear Present,

"We do not heal the past by dwelling there; we heal the past by living fully in the present."

    Marianna Williamson

Dear Future,

Goals

GOALS

> Goal setting helps to develop vision, focus, motivation, and sense of purpose.

My long-terms goals:

1._____

2._____

3._____

4._____

5._____

These are the steps to help me accomplish my long-term goals:

1. _____

   _____

2. _____

   _____

3. _____

   _____

4. _____

   _____

5. _____

   _____

Accomplishing your goals can make you feel proud of yourself. Use this space to reflect on times you felt proud.

I was proud of myself when…

___

These are the things that make me happy:

1._____

2._____

3._____

4._____

5._____

Positive Reflection: Do something you enjoy

Things I am grateful for today:

1._____

2._____

3._____

4._____

5._____

Positive Reflection: Focus on the positive things in life not the negative.

Love

Five things I love about myself:

1._____

2._____

3._____

4._____

5._____

Love
Is Patient, love is kind,
It does not envy,
It does not boast,
It is not proud.
It does not dishonor others,
It is not self-seeking,
It is not easily angered,
It keeps no record of wrongs,
Love does not delight in evil
But rejoices with the truth,
It always protects, always trust,
Always hopes, always perseveres.
Love never fails.
1 Corinthians 13:4-8 NIV

These are ways I have shown love to myself:

1._____

2._____

3._____

4._____

5._____

I am unashamed

Jesus displayed the greatest love for me on the cross. There he took on all my sins. Because of him, I no longer have to be ashamed.

Ashamed: a feeling of being embarrassed or guilty because of your actions.

These are the things I no longer must be ashamed of:

1. _____

2. _____

3. _____

4. _____

5. _____

6. _____

7. _____

8. _____

9. _____

10. _____

Positive Reflection: Forgive yourself for your mistakes.

In my Weakness, God gives me strength.

This was the time in my life that hurt the most but made me the strongest:

Psalm 147:3 He heals the brokenhearted and binds up their wounds.

These are my strengths:

1._____

2._____

3._____

4._____

5._____

These are my weaknesses that I will work on:

1._____

2._____

3._____

4._____

5._____

Positive Reflection: Do not mistake your feelings or insecurities as facts.

Dear Self,

I know that you have experienced some hard times. You have overcome them all and are victorious. I know that you are doing the best that you can and sometimes things get hard. I want you to know that I believe in you. You got this! I love you and I will be with you each step of the way.

Sincerely,

Self-Love

Things I will quit:

1. Doubting myself

2. Quitting

3. Settling

4. Putting myself down

5. _____

6. _____

7. _____

8. _____

9. _____

10. _____

These are the people in my life that have influenced me…

1._____

2._____

3._____

4._____

5._____

Positive Reflection: Write a letter of gratitude to someone who has made an impact in your life.

Prayers...

Complete the blank prayers in your own words.

God, I trust you. I surrender myself, my life and my will to you. Strengthen me that I might become closer to you. Teach me your way and lead me each day. Help me to be who you have created me to be. Help me to love myself and others.

In Jesus Name I pray,

Amen

God, help me to know my purpose. Help me to see myself the way you see me…

Help me to be a woman that inspires others…

There were two women who inspired me growing up. The first was my aunt who was a nurse. I looked up to her. She inspired me to pursue higher education and to be a hard worker. The second was a lady at my church who called me beautiful. She planted a seed in me that took time to grow. That was a truth I did not believe for many years to come.

What women in your life inspire you?

1. _____

2. _____

3. _____

4. _____

5. _____

6. _____

Things that make me beautiful..

   1.
   2.
   3.
   4.
   5.

I am a powerful woman (journal your own thoughts)

_____
_____
_____
_____
_____
_____
_____
_____
_____
_____
_____
_____
_____
_____
_____
_____
_____
_____
_____
_____
_____

Positive Reflection: Spend time with a woman that inspires you.

I will begin to transform my thinking. I will no longer say, "I cannot" and begin to affirm that, "I can."

Use the space below and begin to affirm what you can do.

I can do all things through Christ who gives me strength. Phil 4:13

I know that I have a call on my life. These are the things that God has called me to do.

(If you are unsure, pray and ask him. He speaks!)

1._____

2._____

3._____

4._____

5._____

After asking God what your calling is, take this time to be quiet. Meditate on his word. What is he saying to you? During this time, don't speak just listen. Write down what you hear him say.

Answer the question, "Who Am I?"

Lord, who am I?

Lord who am I?

Where do I turn, where do I go? Lord who am I? Just help me to know.

(God says)

You are my child

I made you especially for me

You were created for my glory and to give me praise

See I loved you so much that I sent my son Jesus to

die for your sins

There's no need to be ashamed any longer

For there is power in his name

Power to heal

Power to save

It is that power that can lead one to change

I know you've faced many challenges

But you are victorious

Yes, victory is your name

Seek your identity through my word

For my child, it will tell you all about my plan and help you to understand

Thanks for the question and thanks for listening

Remember, whenever you need to talk again, I'm here, I'm always listening   -God

These are the negative thoughts I have about myself:

1._____

2._____

3._____

4._____

5._____

6._____

7._____

8._____

9._____

10._____

Exercise: Look in the mirror and read your negative thoughts out loud using an "I am statement" such as, "I am ugly."

Now transform that statement into a positive statement. "I am beautiful"

What God's word says

Ephesians 4:29 *Let no corrupt communication proceed out of your mouth, but that which is good to the use of edifying.*

Do the words you speak to yourself edify and build you up?

_____

_____

_____

_____

_____

_____

_____

_____

_____

_____

_____

_____

_____

_____

_____

2 Corinthians 10:5-7 *Casting down imaginations, and every high thing that exalted itself against the knowledge of God and bring into captivity every thought to the obedience of Christ.*

Examine your thoughts, do they line up with God's word?

_____

_____

_____

_____

_____

_____

_____

_____

_____

_____

_____

_____

_____

Proverbs 18:21 *The tongue has the power of life and death, and those who love it will eat its fruit.*

There is power in the tongue, are you speaking life or death into yourself?

Positive Reflection:

- Replace negative thinking with positive thinking.
- Participate in a physical activity.
- Be kind to yourself.
- Be kind to others.

Five unique things about myself are:

1._____

2._____

3._____

4._____

5._____

Positive Reflection: Don't compare yourself to others.

What I think about myself:

Are these thoughts negative or positive?

Where did these thoughts come from? My parents, friends, experiences, or God's word?

When negative thoughts come into your mind, think to yourself…

Is it true?

Are these thoughts necessary?

Do they line up with God's word?

Do they make me feel good?

Will they help me as a person?

Circle your strengths

- Ambitious
- Courageous
- Creative
- Caring
- Disciplined
- Determined
- Empathetic
- Encouraging
- Forgiving
- Honest
- Kind

I will not compare myself to others; I will cultivate who I am.

I Deserve (Use this space to write down what you believe you deserve)

_____
_____
_____
_____
_____
_____
_____
_____
_____
_____
_____
_____
_____
_____
_____
_____
_____
_____
_____
_____
_____

You deserve love, honesty and respect.

These are the things I am thankful for today:

1._____

2._____

3._____

4._____

5._____

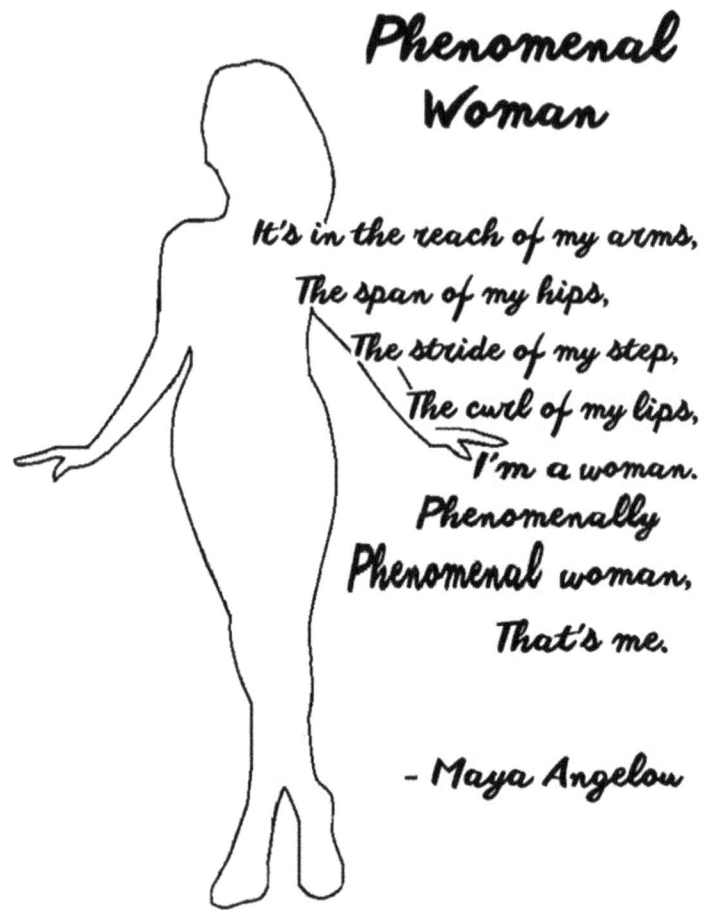

Phenomenal Woman

It's in the reach of my arms,
The span of my hips,
The stride of my step,
The curl of my lips,
I'm a woman.
Phenomenally
Phenomenal woman,
That's me.

- Maya Angelou

I give myself permission to:

1. Believe what God's word says about me.
2. Love myself.
3. Walk in my calling.
4. Forgive myself.
5. Forgive others.
6. Be me.

"You cannot be who you are not.

Eventually you will no longer fool yourself."

#MsBeautifulThought

God's Truth

"For I know the plans I have for you, declares the Lord. Plans to prosper you and not to harm you, plans to give you hope and a future. Then you will call on me and come and pray to me, and I will listen to you. You will seek me and find me when you seek me with all your heart. I will be found by you," declares the lord.

Jeremiah 29:11-14

God is within me. I will not fail.

Psalms 46:5

What does Proverbs 31 say about a woman?

Read Jeremiah 1:5, When does it say that God knew you?

What did God make beautiful in Ecclesiastes 3:11?

_____

_____

Does this include you?

_____

What do these verses mean to you?

_____

_____

_____

_____

_____

_____

_____

_____

_____

_____

_____

_____

_____

_____

_____

_____

These are the stories of individuals who felt unloved, unwanted, alienated or inadequate...

1. I've been beat more times than I can remember. Age 56

2. I was burned when I was a baby by a pot of hot grease. Burns cover 90% of my body. I was talked about as a child. Age 38

3. My mother is Caucasian, and my father is African American. Growing up, I never felt like I connected to either race. I did not know where I fit in. Age 28

4. Sometimes I feel sad and all alone. Age 37

5. I have been told that I am just like my mother who is on drugs and that I will never amount to anything. Age 40

6. I am smaller and shorter than my friends. Sometimes I wish God made me taller. I wish he made me different. Age 11

7. I am taller than my friends, my hair is short and thick. I don't look like other kids in my grade. Age 13

8. My mother couldn't take care of me when I was a baby, so I went to live with my father. Now that I am an adult, I spend my life taking care of my adult siblings. Sometimes I feel invisible. Age 37

9. Sometimes I lie to get attention. I tell kids things that are not true. I am learning that I do not have to lie to make people like me. Age 14

10. Sometimes I experience so much pain in my body that I don't want to leave the bed for days. My family refuses to help me. Age 38

11. At birth I had a stroke and I only have use of one hand. Growing up, I couldn't do things like other kids could do like play basketball or other sports. Age 60

12. I have been mean to other kids. I am the school bully, but it is the only place I get attention. Nobody pays attention to me at home. Age 13

13. I have been divorced twice. Often time I wonder if I will ever experience real love. Age 40

14. I had an abortion and wonder if God will forgive me. Age 25

You have just read about men, women and children who have at one point felt like they were unloved, unwanted, alienated or inadequate. We all have a different story, but no matter your story, we are all enough and loved by God. Never allow your story or your past to hold you hostage and keep you from believing God's truth about you.

"I am"

...are two of the most powerful words.

You are the one to determine what comes after them.

(In this section, repeat each I Am statement and meditate on it. Write them down several times or simply use the lines to reflect your own thoughts)

I am powerful beyond measure.

I am strong and courageous.

I am beautiful.

I am powerful.

I deserve love.

I am important.

I am wanted.

I am qualified.

I am called by God to do good things.

I am chosen.

I will not allow others to keep me locked in my past. I am forgiven.

I am enough (was there ever a time you felt inadequate?)

My past has no power over me.

I am worthy.

I am favored.

I am growing into who God called me to be.

I am victorious.

I was born with purpose.

I am needed.

I will succeed.

I forgive myself.

I was born for such a time as this. Esther 4:14

I am a blessing to others. I will be the lender and not the borrower.

I believe what God's word says about me.

I am a conqueror.

I am brave.

I am faithful.

I am fearfully and wonderfully made.

I am beautiful (was there ever a time you did not feel this way?)

I will not allow my past or my present to determine my future.

I am no longer the victim.

I am blessed and highly favored.

I am taking off my mask and showing the world who I really am.

I am unashamed.

I matter.

I am loved.

I walk in integrity.

I can do all things through Christ who gives me strength.

I am worth the wait.

I am worthy of love.

I am no longer ashamed of my past.

Now that you have began the journey of self-discovery and healing, allow the negative opinions of others and your own insecurities to become a part of your past. As God begins to reveal your worth and identity to you, help someone else to see it in themselves. I encourage you to embrace your present with confidence.

Dear Past,

_____

_____

_____

_____

_____

_____

_____

_____

_____

Signed.

X_____

My Motivation

The question, "Who Am I" has been asked throughout this book. I too as you all have read, have had to ask myself this question. This question has been asked throughout my life. When I was molested as a child, when I found out that I had three siblings that I had never met, when I became a teen mom, when my first husband and I divorced, even when I gave my life to God, this has always been my question. If I am asking this question, how many other women are asking this same question?

There are several factors that motivated me to create this workbook. My own struggles and challenges within myself as a youth and an adult, the young ladies I encountered working at a homeless shelter for pregnant teens, my time as a foster care worker working with teens who were apart of sex trafficking, who experienced feeling rejected and unwanted and my time teaching at a women's rehab center. How do these women learn how to heal from their hurts and walk in their identity? This was the question that I pondered. With that question and by the leading of the holy spirit, this workbook was birthed.

I can proudly say, that I am no longer the victim, that is my truth. Who am I? I am powerful, strong, loved, enough and most importantly, God's child.

My desire is that women will work through this journal/workbook and be able to proclaim that as well. It is my goal that a portion of the profits will allow this book to get into the hands of women who need it most.

Let's help other women to realize their worth and identity.

www.ingramcontent.com/pod-product-compliance
Lightning Source LLC
Chambersburg PA
CBHW071510040426
42444CB00008B/1581